A Saving Grace

BOOKS BY LORNA CROZIER

Inside Is the Sky 1976
Crow's Black Joy 1979
Humans and Other Beasts 1980
No Longer Two People (with Patrick Lane) 1981
The Weather 1983
The Garden Going On Without Us 1985
Angels of Flesh, Angels of Silence 1988
Inventing the Hawk 1992
Everything Arrives at the Light 1995

A Saving Grace

THE COLLECTED POEMS OF MRS. BENTLEY

by

LORNA CROZIER

CANADIAN CATALOGUING IN PUBLICATION DATA

Crozier, Lorna, 1948–
  A saving grace: the collected poems of Mrs. Bentley

ISBN 0-7710-2480-0

I. Title.

PS8555.R72S38 1996   C811'.54   C96-931087-0
PR9199.3.C76S38 1996

The publishers acknowledge the support of the Canada
Council and the Ontario Arts Council for their publishing
program.

Typesetting by M&S, Toronto
Printed and bound in Canada

McClelland & Stewart Inc.
The Canadian Publishers
481 University Avenue
Toronto, Ontario
M5G 2E9

1 2 3 4 5   00 99 98 97 96

In memory of Sinclair Ross (1908-1996).

And for my mother, Peggy Crozier,
who tells me her stories.

Saturday Evening, April 8

Above, in the high cold night, the wind goes swinging past, indifferent, liplessly mournful. It frightens me, makes me feel lost, dropped on this little perch of town and abandoned. I wish Philip would waken.

> – Mrs. Bentley, in *As For Me and My House*
>   by Sinclair Ross

Behold, the Lord maketh the earth empty, and maketh it waste, and turneth it upside down. . . .

> – Isaiah 24:1

A Man and a Woman

Wind blows from the west.
In a double bed a man and woman
lie side by side, pretending sleep.
Breathe in, breathe out.
When he feels me move, he rolls over,
turns his face to the wall.
Why don't I tell him it's okay?
I know he's awake, I can't
touch him, can't speak.
My hand would have to separate
from my body to reach for him.
A country lies between us, a prairie
winter, years and years of drought.
When did it begin?
Wind blows from the west.
Surely even in this dusty room,
this marriage bed,
the small rain down will rain.

In the Open

No place to lose yourself,
no trees. The wheat in the fields
where children used to hide
is stunted, barely reaching my knees.

On Main Street
wind has pushed the buildings
back on either side;
now there's room for it
to shoulder through.

At night with the dog
I leave the house.
The light from Philip's window
falls thin and narrow across the yard.

I walk along the railroad tracks,
long blue lines electric in the moonlight
pulling the horizon suddenly near.

El Greco runs ahead
then stops,

lopes back if I lag too far behind,
till he takes off, baying,
that wonderful sound he was born to.

He won't come back till hours
later, a scratch at the door,
paws torn from prickly pears
padding the hills.

In the open I stand
in the darkness a field makes,
nothing around
my body, nothing touching it
except the night I draw inside,
breath after breath.

I must teach myself
what the dog already knows,
find what I was born to,
though gladness is gone
from the earth
and there is no light in me,
there is no music.

Two Eternal Things

Early summer, the land wanting
colour – sienna, gamboge,
burnt umber – Philip says,
making a joke of it,
he'll paint a thistle
against a rock.

Two eternal things
in this godforsaken place:
rock – what the drought
cannot destroy,
thistle – what the grasshoppers
will not eat.

Call it *Hope*, I say.
Despair, he replies.

BUMPER CROP

Everyone talks of '27,
wild grass greening the pastures,
bushes plush with berries
and best of all, the bumper crop.
A preacher would have had it good
then too. *As ye sow so shall ye reap.*
The fruits of your labour, et cetera,
every sermon rolling off the tongue
like grain into the bin.
Now Philip prays for rain
and nothing happens
or the rainfall comes too late.

Even in the bottom of the coulees
where creeks used to run
cows graze on dust and thistles,
the little milk they give
thin and blue. Above them
horses drag their hunger
like a plow made out of bones.

When I walk by the fields
I try to imagine the bumper crop –
wheat so tall and golden
it floats above the mind.
Grass rises to a horse's belly,
and every Sunday Philip cries
Everyone that thirsteth,
come ye to the waters,
come, buy wine and milk
without money, without price.

CYCLES

I had hoped for something else,
a small stirring
in the deepest part of me
a moon-ghost flutter
thin as the wingbone
of a wish.

Some days a woman's body is blood
and gravity, the lower half
heavy as a rusted bell
sinking in the mud.

It has been there since my birth
though the darkest notes
have yet to reach me.

Made of iron, they move so slow.

COUNTRY DWELLER

Paul, the school teacher
who drops by to see us
now and then, tells me
pagan means *country dweller* –
that's where we've gone wrong.
We've tried to tame the wild gods
and make them one.

Maybe even Philip
could believe in them.
A horse god. Among the reeds
and rushes, a wind god.
In aspen leaves, a god of light.

The smallest, the most slender
is the god of rain.

I tell Paul she must be
female, a four-legged animal
with soft paws and swishing tail

for that's what we hear
when she comes near us
for her green communion
with the grass.

Names

The town has every kind of person
and a name for everyone. The boy
who shovels grain at the elevator
and who cannot hear or speak
is Dummy Martin. The butcher's daughter
who sells skinned rabbits
door-to-door and who's simple
in the head, Silly Prior.

Gimpy Bisset is the blacksmith
who lost his leg in the War;
Dong, the honey-wagon man.
When he was a kid
a wheel ran over the side
of his head, now shaped
strangely like a bell.

All the Ukrainians are Bohunks
and the tinker who drives into town
to mend the pots,

sharpen knives and scissors,
The Dirty Jew.

Yesterday, out with the dog,
I talked to the woman who lives
in the cook car abandoned by the CPR
at the edge of town. I admired
the baby she was fanning with her hat
to keep the flies away
though he's a homely little thing.

Her husband's Smiley Mitchell.
Too proud to stand in line for relief,
he's small and mean and wears a stupid grin.
When she was pregnant, she told me,
all she had to eat were eggs
her mother sent from the farm.

Every night for six months,
before Smiley stumbled home,
she knocked at the café's back door.
Woo Chow gave her a bowl of chop suey,
the piece of pie no one bought

and all the tea she could drink.
"He's better than most of them,"
she said. "He's a good Chink,
but I daren't tell my husband
what I done."

Dust

Rags stuffed under the doors,
around the windows
as if they were wounds
that needed staunching

yet the dust
settles everywhere,
on my skin, my hair, inside
my sleeves and collar.
I feel old, used up,
something found
in the back of a cupboard.

I cover the water crock
with a tea towel
embroidered with a *B*,
turn the dinner plates
face down on the table.
When we lift them
two moons glow
on the gritty cloth

and in the mornings when we rise,
the shape of our heads
remains on the pillowslips
as if we leave behind
the part of us
that keeps on dreaming.

CONFESSION

When I praise him
Philip tells me to turn
his drawings upside down.

It's not the likenesses
of the faces, the stingy houses,
in his sketches of the town
but the formal composition –
that's what I must look for.

I've never said it
but there's something missing,
something about this place
he hasn't caught.

Even the horses he painted
at the river lack the wild
beauty of being simply *horse*,
a horse's girth and sinews,
the heave of its chest
as it runs the meadows.

His hand is connected
only to his eye
as if he were the god
who's forsaken all his creatures
and brings them back
in hard strokes on paper,
forgetting the blood
that courses through them

forgetting what his hands
must have felt
as he pulled them from the mud,
as he placed his mouth
with its smell of swamps and heaven
over their nostrils,
as he breathed.

THE EGG

In the middle of the table
Paul places an egg
as if there were a world inside,
a universe of light. I pick it up
and wipe it with my apron.
It's been a while since I've seen one,
most of the hens not laying.

We'll play crib, he says,
to see who gets to eat it.
The winner must not share.

When have I played for higher stakes,
such sweet anticipation?

A soft-boiled egg, five minutes in the pot,
the top lopped off,
a pinch of salt and pepper,
one slice of bread, homemade,
to dip into the yolk.

He says he'll stay till I eat each bit
and lick the spoon – I'm not allowed
to save a bite for Philip.

Fifteen-two, fifteen-four, fifteen-six,
I must watch him closely so he doesn't
let me win. I've no rights to it.

In the kerosene glow of the lamp
we light at noon
the egg sits between us,
unbearably mysterious and whole.

The Kind of Woman

Yesterday they found Emma Humphreys
at the bottom of the dry well
on the neighbour's farm. Mrs. Bird
says there's no way she could have
fallen in. It was deliberate.
She threw herself and the baby
into the darkness and lay there
for three days until Rusty Howes
lowered a lantern on a rope
to take a look inside.
Just a hunch, he said.

When he saw her there,
the baby still and white as wax,
he didn't know if the kindest thing
was to walk away. But his brothers
eased him down, hand over hand,
to bring her up, still alive,
saying nothing, a dead
look in her eyes.
Her husband took her home.

He seems a decent man
but what goes on in houses
when no one's there
but family? A man,
a baby and his wife.

Dr. Bird said it was amazing
nothing was broken.

The church women at Mrs. Finley's
over tea wondered what kind of woman
would do a thing like that?
I wish I'd said the kind of woman
like you, like me

but I changed the subject
to next Sunday's hymns, afraid
if I talked of her, the darkness
she found more comforting than light,
I'd say too much. Who knows
what makes a woman leap
into a well with her baby,
lie there for three days –

that small death in her arms –

and not call out,
not call out,
for her own good reason
not wanting to be found.

ALL THE ROOM YOU NEED

Sky: an eye that never blinks.
So much pain in me some days
I bend double under its gaze,
each vertebra a stone.
This is what comes of being
too much alone. There's no end
to it here, the sky gives you
all the room you need
to grow small.

BEAUTY

In this place what does a word
like *beauty* mean? This morning
Mrs. Holly in a freshly laundered dress,
a green ribbon flirting with
her wavy auburn hair.
She stopped by to talk to Philip,
about Sunday School, she claimed.

I answered the door in an old dress
and scuffed slippers, the toes wet.
I'd been scrubbing floors, dirty-
water bracelets around my wrists.

In the parlour with Philip
she leaned towards his chair,
touched the air around him
with her hands, frail and white
and lightly freckled. I hid mine
deep in my apron pockets,
tucked my feet beneath its folds.

Later Philip told me it was my own fault
for not being more presentable.
In a preacher's house
you never know who'll drop by.
Someone fussier than Jesus,
I might have said.

There are days when I find myself
almost beautiful. My hands
large and sure across piano keys,
my arms firm from carrying pails of water
and breaking kindling in the shed
at night so the neighbours won't see
another sign of Philip's weakness.

If he were strong,
if he could show me any tenderness,
my hands would be that delicate,
they'd braid green ribbons through my hair.

Wind

We have all seen it here –
its ribs pressed into snow
and drifts of topsoil
smothering the fence lines.

It never passes by
but prowls outside the house,
an animal
come down from hunger.

It's what drives the women crazy
especially on the farms
it never stops.

It can strip a roof,
clap a barn to the ground,
crack a windmill like a wishbone.
You have to tilt to walk into it,
your body lists. All your words
are nothing in its mouth.

Some days it stops you dead
and suddenly
you've run out of time,
your life swept behind you
and the wind in front
not letting you
take another step.

One Willow Grows

By the dried-up creek one willow grows.
It knows how to douse from emptiness
its red wands, its drowsy tongues.
Bless me, for I have sinned.
I have cared too much for the rain.
I have made for her a golden idol
from sheaves of wheat. Bless me, wind.
Bless me, dust. Bless me, willow.
How far in the darkness your roots must travel
to send such speaking to the light.

Another story. This time
the husband, home a night early,
leans in the bedroom doorway,
freshly painted. His wife thinks
she dreams his shadow huge above her
as she sleeps in the arms
of his friend. The next morning
the neighbours find him frozen on his knees,
not far from the house. He clutches
barbed wire, blood around his hands
hard as beads
and when they cut him free,
bring his body to her, she sees
on his palm a streak of paint.

What's the moral of this tale?

Woman, you will suffer
for your infidelities,
be justly punished. Women,
appreciate your big silent men,

speak to them, learn to listen
though their words are thick and clumsy,
hands blunt as blocks of wood.

Woman, there is no forgiveness.

Don't paint doors
or leave them open,
don't believe you dream.

Playing Liszt

The closest I came to Steve –
the orphan who lived with us
too short a time – was the night
I played for him, my reasons
far from pure. I wanted Philip
to know he couldn't hold him.

They say in a storm when dust
blows against wire fences,
the barbs spark. If you're lost
and can't see in front of you
follow the thorns of light
and you'll make it home.

That night my fingers sparked on ivory.
For a moment what was good
in the boy and me,
what was graceful, without guile,
found a home together
however brief – even the dog
we'd lose within the month

as we'd lose Steve
trembled with the joy of it,
his yellow eyes on fire.

The Dance

Light on his feet
the cowboy took me in his arms
and we danced
"Let Me Call You Sweetheart,"
then a wild schottische
where he and his buddy
swung me so fast
my heels grew wings.

At intermission he asked me
to come see his horse
and I went, hoping Philip
would watch me leave,
but it was Paul who saw me,
told me later I was a fool.

In the barn that particular
warmth you get only
from a large animal's body,
the hay-sweet smell,
the soft muzzle in my palm.

And that is all we did –
we looked at his horse.

But before we went back
he lead me to a wooden box
packed with straw. Inside,
six puppies, red-brown and fat,
spilled over one another,
backs saliva-wet, all touch,
lick and spittle

and I wanted to cry,
my skin longing for the warm
baptism of tongues.

BURIAL, PARTRIDGE HILL

I've never seen the dust
this bad. The world
turns upside down, the sky's
the earth. Among the graves
badgers dig their way to heaven.

After the service Mrs. Lawson cries
she wants no one who belongs to her
left in this place.

Her husband tells her
he'll sink chicken wire
around the coffin, six feet deep
and four feet long.

Five years of being burnt out,
blown out, hailed out,
and now they plant
their only son.

SKINNING HORSES

No one wants to do what Alex does.
It's horses he's after, the dead
who starved in winter pastures,
their hides worth three bucks each.

Only Paul will sit with him,
his wife and daughters in the pew
just behind the organ.
The true outcasts in this town
though few will talk to Dong,
Woo Chow, or Ephraim, unless
there's business to be done.

Early mornings when I'm out walking
I've seen him with his team and wagon
creaking through the countryside.
El Greco wants to follow but I grab him
by the scruff of his neck
and wait for them to pass.

I try not to imagine his hands,
the slick work they do

to keep his family clothed and fed,
that stench all around him.
They say it's soaked into his flesh,
it's on his wife and children,
but there's never been a man
with cleaner hands.

I've heard he scrubs each day
with a brush soaked in vanilla
bought from the Watkins man in bulk.
That's what I smell at the organ,
a faint whiff around his family
like when I bake a custard or a cake.

Now when I measure a teaspoon of vanilla
I can't help but see
those huge flayed bodies
and the bloody muzzles of the farm dogs
who follow Alex and his wagon
like gulls that swoop and dive behind a plow.

Not the Music

Not the music.
It is this other thing
I keep from all of them
that matters, inviolable.

I scratch in my journals,
a mouse rummaging through cupboards,
nibbling on a crust of bread, apple skins,
chewing the edges of photographs, the small
details of a life. I hoard and save,
place one thing inside another
inside the next.

Start with the prairie, then Horizon
and inside it our house,
the kitchen, the table where I sit
with my journal, and inside it
everything I write – dust, moths,
wind speaking in whispers
across the page,
the absence of rain,

forgiveness –
everything shrinking
to the smallest
thinnest letter,
I.

Refrain

O Philip, who doesn't even dance,
who wrote you into this story?
This refrain of dust, dust, dust,
and nothing ever touching
but the wind
day after day without meaning,
without love.

Fox

So hot, the heat punches you
and the railroad tracks
burn the soles of your shoes.
My first morning out in days,
I feel something watching me
and turn to see a fox. *Sister,*
I say without thinking,
and she seems to understand.
Her eyes are green leaves,
wet on the underside,
deep pools of grass
I wade into,
rain suddenly so thick
it casts a shadow as it falls.

GARDEN

Out of the blue
while he helps me
carry water to the garden,
Paul says *breast*
used to rhyme with *priest*.

This is quite daring for him
and I wonder what to make of it.
He claims two hundred years ago
the pronunciation changed
to the way we say it now.
Another theory is that *breast*
comes from *brustian*,
to *bud* or *sprout*.

I make a joke about the garden,
say it's more like a priest,
the rows of seedlings
abstemious and thin. Paul
smiles, but nervously.
We've gone too far.

When I go inside to wash my hands,
   (*I will water thee with my tears*)
I can feel my nipples hard against my dress.
I rub them with my thumb. Neglected,

it only takes a word for me
to bud and moisten, brustian
Mrs. B in her celibate garden.

COMFORT ME

Comfort me with apples,
for I am sick with love.
Comfort me with sweet grass
wound around your fingers
for I am sick with love.
Let me follow the antelope's
trails into the pastures
of your flesh, let me lie
where the graceful one is sleeping,
suckle the bud that never blooms,
for I am sick with love.
Lo, winter is past,
the seeds have been scattered
and the rains do not come.

JOE LAWSON'S WIFE

The woman who pounded on our door
came out of the wind, hair wild,
voice thin and broken. Philip
drove with Dr. Bird beside him,
I sat in the back with her,
Joe Lawson's wife, both of us silent
and staring straight ahead
though there was nothing to see
in those two beams of light. How
to comfort? When we got to the barn,
Philip was awkward with the rope.
The doctor pushed him aside,
climbed the milking-stool
the man had kicked away
and cut him down. Joe Lawson,
though it was hard to call
what hung in the barn
that name – the rope had cut into his neck,
his face blue and bloated.

I kept my eyes on his hands.
They were what you noticed
when you first saw Joe. Big, solid hands,
as much a part of the land as the stones
ice heaves from the earth every spring.

It was a minister they needed
not the doctor, but Philip hung back.
Dr. Bird was the one who told me
Take her to the house and make some tea.
She wouldn't leave,
but covered her man with a blanket
that smelled of horse, then sat
in the dirty straw, his swollen head
in her lap. By then her sister had arrived
and the neighbour with a wagon.
The sun was rising, its splinters
from the cracks in the walls
falling all around her.

At last she let the men
carry the body from the barn
but still wouldn't go.

She pulled the wooden stool
to the stall and milked the cow,
its udder heavy, barn cats
coming out of nowhere at the sound.

There was no pail,
milk streamed out and hit the ground,
pooled around her feet,
the cats licking and mewling.
Her sister stood helplessly beside her
and motioned us away.
There was nothing to do but go,
above her head Philip mumbling
something I couldn't hear.

At home, he clung to me
as if his feet were swinging through the air
and it was I that held him up.
How to comfort. We bring so little
to each other. Later, after we had slept
he went into his study and I followed,
watched him from the door.
So upset, he left it open.

He tore the drawings he had sketched
last Sunday, his parishioners
as he had seen them from the pulpit – all
alike, his pencil strokes relentless,
pinning them and their piety to the pews.

Everything would change for us
if he could draw
that woman on her stool, her simple
act of courage – or was it resignation?
The shadow of her husband still
swaying from the rafters,
milk puddling at her feet
and between the cracks,
the sun's bright nails pounding through.

I Feed on Thistles

I feed on thistles,
I mourn like the dove.
My neck is a barbed sinew,
my brow brass. I have graven
you on the palms of my hands.
I have made bare my holy arms.
I will make the place
of my breasts glorious.
For a small moment
I have forsaken you,
but with great mercies
I will gather you in.
I will make fat thy bones,
you will be a watered garden.
I will tend you I will make
of you a harvest, the fruit
of my body will be sweet
on your lips,
will moisten your mouth,
will glisten you.

STATE OF GRACE

All things must pass, twelve years
of marriage, five of drought.
But what's to be done with beauty,
the bewildering presence of love?
Because the air is thick with dust
the sky burns red at sunset,
meadows of poppies and wild roses.
Paul brings me sweet peas, small
and fragrant from his mother's garden.
Though she is seventy she waters them
from a spring, walking a mile
with her bucket, there and back,
careful not to spill. Last night
the sky was green as an unripe
peach, its skin peeled away,
revealing what lies beneath it – not
darkness but streams of light,
the Aurora Borealis, leaping.
Philip and I watched from the step,

holding hands, the whole sky dancing,
and we beneath it, a state of grace.
For the first time I could imagine
life without him.

Sins of Omission

Things I didn't mention
in my journal:

toiletries, relatives, bankers,
favourite books, hobos, yeast infections,
wire worms, cut worms, wheat rust,
relief lines at the station, the Curse,
flour-sack pyjamas, Russian thistles, salt cod,
masturbation, Depression cake (no butter, no
eggs), well-witchers, buffalo stones, what came out
of me that night, chinook arches, grasshopper
plagues, the white enamel pan Philip
carried to the garden, Bennett buggies,
chokecherries, burying what was in it,
box socials, potato moonshine,
where nothing grows

WINTER HORSES

The horses pull into town
white with hoarfrost, huge
albino beasts from a fairy tale.

In my dreams I ride one
under a cold and flawless moon.
Nothing moves me
but this animal between my legs.

He knows where we are going
and takes me there
past the houses where everyone's asleep,
above the elevators, suddenly small.

When we cross the sky's great lake
black with ice, his hooves
strike sparks big as stars.

LAUGHTER FALLS LIKE RAIN

Paul drops in from the Chinaman's,
he's had a laugh or two, the men
telling stories over coffee.
Because the sky's full of dirt
Caswell says he's throwing seeds
into the air this spring.
Slim McMurchie claims his wife
keeps a box of gophers
by the stove, tosses one out the door
every Monday morning. If it starts
digging before it hits the ground,
she doesn't hang her washing on the line.
Even Woo Chow who rarely smiles
said he heard one of the Nagel boys
from out Leader way
got lost rounding second base
in last summer's dust storm
and hasn't been seen since.
Such saving grace, these stories.
When Philip hears us laughing,
he slams the door he left half open,

and Paul, ever polite,
says he's got work to do and goes.
I must find a way to see
what's funny here,
in this House of Bentley, cry
till I laugh and laugh,
the sweet rain coming down.

WHAT WORDS ARE LEFT

Paul shows me his collection
of immigration pamphlets
meant to attract settlers
to the West. "Notice," he says,
"the writers weren't allowed
to use the word *cold*."
Weather became *Invigorating*.
Healthful. Fresh.

Imagine! It would be like
being forbidden to say
wind in this place,
or *dust*, or *loneliness*.
What words are left?

Cold, cold, cold,
I want to shout it!

Some winters
the noses of the cattle bleed.
Farm cats lose the tips of

ears and tails.
Between house and barn,
lost in a blizzard
a man can freeze solid
as a chunk of poplar.

Behind the elevator
by the tracks last February
I found the small black
triangle of a kitten's ear
lying on the snow
like a piece of tin,
thin and brittle. I
picked it up, placed it
between the pages of my book.

A winter petal,
emblem of the season,
this country's harsh, un-
erasable word.

JUDITH

It's taken me this long to write it:
Judith. A strong biblical name
for such a girl. I should say
woman, Miss Judith West.

  I am my beloved's, and my beloved is mine.

That night I moved through my fever
as if it were a house; remember
the game you played as a child?
Lying on your back in bed you stared
till the ceiling became the floor.
You stepped over a ledge
through the doorway, circled
the lightbulb, stem tall as a tulip's.

  *The beams of our house are of cedar
  and our rafters of fir.*

That's where I was, on the ceiling,
looking down. They weren't in the woodshed,

as I said, in that smell of dog
and kindling, but in the kitchen,
everything scrubbed and shining and
reflecting light. It made it worse somehow,
in my kitchen. He sat naked on a chair.
She straddled him.

He feedeth among the lilies.

I seemed to float above their heads
though I could clearly see
the swell and gleam of her buttocks
and hear him groan.

*I am my beloved's
and his desire is towards me.*

My whole body ached
not with the pain of fever but
a deeper hurt, less centred.
If I'd been a different woman
I would have screamed, raked my nails
down her back.

Who is she that looketh forth
as the morning, fair as the moon,
clear as the sun, and terrible
as an army with banners?

I moved my legs and arms
like an underwater swimmer
and made it to our bed. The dog,
hearing them, scratched at the door,
whimpering. Or was it me?

This is my beloved,
and this is my friend,
O daughters of Jerusalem.

In the morning I thought
I made the whole thing up,
but Philip was too kind to me.

His left hand should be under my head
and his right hand should embrace me.

And when he left
to buy something special

for my breakfast, I climbed out of bed,
stumbled through the kitchen
to the door. On hands and knees,
I followed with my fingers
the dog's claw tracks in the wood,
an exegesis white as scars,
and I saw everything again
as I had seen it –

   his belly bright ivory,
   his legs pillars of marble
   set upon sockets of fine gold,
   this is my beloved

the marrow in my bones aching.

HAWK AND RABBIT

The sky is made for hawks.
Their screams come from deep inside,
a long glistening vein
pulled from my gut, stretched into sound.

Yesterday I watched one
take a rabbit
and felt no sentiment. I, too,
want to sink into something soft,

tear and rend, all that
tenderness ripped apart,
the rabbit – my heart –
with its leaps and sudden terror.

BAG OF ORANGES

If her family had been better off
she'd have gone to Saskatoon
"to visit an aunt." That's what
they called it then, aunt or no.
Here I've heard the locals say,
"She's gone visiting a Model T,"
because it probably happened
in the back seat.
Judith's family was dirt poor.
Nothing for her to do
but go back to the farm,
pretending she was ill.

No one guessed the father
though every name in town
came up except the preacher's.
I sent Philip to the farm –
I'm not sure why,
gave him a sack of oranges,
insisting he tell her

they were a gift from me.
I packed them in hay
so they wouldn't bruise.
I wanted them
round and hard and sweet.

That morning when I watched him
ride away, I wished he'd leave for good,
do something brave and true for once.
Then I panicked at the thought.
Who am I if not Mrs. Bentley?

When he returned, I asked him how she was.
Don't send oranges again, he said.
She wept and wept in the kitchen chair,
holding one in each hand.

After supper, before he could go
to his study, close the door,
I said, We'll help her out.
We'll take her baby. (I couldn't bear
the joy flickering across his face.)
It's the Christian thing to do.

Poor Philip who has tasted
the waters of Paradise,
the sip small and brief.
If she is a fruit full and ripening,
I am a gourd with hard
and bitter seeds.

THIS IS THE CHILD

Nailed to a tree,
sliced with a knife
high on the hill,
thrown in a dry well,
buried in the wheat,
drowned in a baptism of pain.

This is the child I bore you.

Like a sow I crushed him,
like a rabbit I ate him,
like a father I cast him out,
like a mother I rose from my bed
and searched out his cry,
my breasts the dugs of a dog.

I should have fed the mouth of God:
my flesh is his sparrow,
my sex the hive of his kingdom,
my hair the thatch to cover my shame.

Milk and honey run from my nipples
and down my thighs
but the child will not come
to me again.

Buffalo Stone

Our arms can't meet around it,
Paul's and mine. White as a skull,
splattered with orange and yellow lichen,
it anchors the sky above the river.

Here the many buffalo walked round,
scratching matted backs.
Huffing and snorting in the sun
they polished the edges
smooth. Paul takes my hand,
runs my fingers along the shine.
I can feel oil from the hides,
smell the sage they rubbed into stone.

Joe Cuthand who breaks broncos at the ranch
said the herds moved underground,
graze just beneath our feet.
If you press your ear against the grass
you can hear them breathing.

If his people keep on dancing
the earth will part like the sea

and the buffalo rumble out,
swinging their heads free of the dark.

Barefoot I follow the sunken circle
round the stone, bearing such a weight.
Here I can almost believe
it's not too late. If I dance
through the long dead seasons

I'll rise one spring
on the back of a massive old bull,
dust streaming from my hair,
around us, the thunder of mothers
and newborn calves, their hooves
storming the hills.

LATE AFTERNOON

For the first time I walk the tracks
without El Greco. I want to believe
he loved the wildness
the coyotes called out of him
before they dragged him down.

Late afternoon, the light is waiting
with the patience a body knows
when it is just beginning
to understand time. Each stone,
each clod of earth has a dark twin
holding it still.

Crossing the open, light moves
low to the ground
like a hound on a rabbit trail;
at home in his flesh
he makes his spirit visible
as breath in winter.

What must be El Greco
doubles back as wind,

mouths my coat and whines.
He tugs me around the bend
where something waits,
something shimmers.

It could be coyote,
it could be the light's
tawny muscles that heave
into the sky
what I won't let go.

PAUL

I made him promise
not to say a word.
And I wrote nothing down.

I wanted it to be
unreadable.

He met me underneath
the trestle, in the coulee's dip.
Both of us were clumsy, he
from inexperience, I guess,
me too long out of use.

This is the funny part –
Paul, the philologist,
was very good with his tongue.

When I came
there was no roar of
a train overhead, no
jealous husband on the ties

looking down. *Paul,*
I said out loud,
twice, so I wouldn't
trick myself
and he felt good inside me,
as good as   any man

though afterwards
we couldn't look at one another.

I walked through town
my blouse buttoned wrong
and didn't know it
till Philip undid the buttons,
did them up again,
under the cotton my skin burning.

I was peeling potatoes
at the kitchen sink.
When he touched me
the knife slipped –
flames spilling from my finger.
I burnt my mouth with its heat.

How Beautiful Upon the Earth

Someone strides ahead of me,
blue robes snapping,
feet bound with winding sheets of dust.
I have sat in the riverbed,
I have come down, I have bent
like willows by the watercourses.

Owls with blind eyes
nest in my womb for it is empty.
No more will I be called
tender and delicate, no more
will I be barren.
I uncover my thigh, bare
the hollow and the wound.
Someone walks the fields.

I have sat in the dust,
I am weeping, I am a woman
of unclean lips. Place the burning
in my mouth that I may speak.
How beautiful upon the earth
the feet of him who comes to me.

Take an harp, go about the city,
thou harlot that has been forgotten;
make sweet melody, sing many songs,
that thou mayest be remembered.

Mater Dolorosa

In April, everyone talking of seeding,
Judith West, whose voice in the choir
rose like a benediction above the wind,
gives birth in a field of mud and melting snow,
flocks of geese crying overhead.

If she were a proper heroine
next day she'd die.

To Philip then she'd be *Saint* Judith.
Nothing I could do but die myself,
meet a train around the bend,
in my pocket a note: *I know everything!*

Instead I tell him once again
I want the baby –
the preacher and his wife
their sister's keeper.
The House of Bentley, we will
serve the Lord.

What was promised was a son
and now we have him,
made from dust and spittle,
carried by a wild goose
above the roofs, the fallow fields,
to this good woman's arms.

WILDERNESS

Like Mrs. Moodie I could say
the wilderness moved inside me
but where there is no bush,
the wilderness is different.

It's really space that rushes at you
in spite of fences, the grid roads
laid in graphs across the earth.

A space not as empty as
you might imagine, it's a thing itself
minus details you can't separate
the whole into any parts.
The worst is

            it doesn't need you.
It goes on and on whether the land
is broken or not, whether a town makes
its small exclamation mark or flattens out.

What's most like the prairie
is the mind of God, the huge way

he must have of looking at the world.
That's why I feel small and scared
inside myself, and yet at times
full of wonder.

LEAVING

This time it's the Bairds.
No one expected to see them go –
his dad had homesteaded
so he owned the place outright.
Philip drove out to say goodbye
and talked to the wife.
She said it was the horses
finally broke them.

He'd built a herd of ten from a team
his dad had brought from North Dakota,
kept them alive with what little feed
he could find. He'd never say
how attached he was,
what man would, she asked,
but you could tell by the way
he stroked their necks and spoke to them
when no one was around.

One of them died of sleeping sickness.
Baird strapped slings of canvas

with ropes at both ends
under the horses' bellies,
strung the ropes over the beams
to keep the horses off their feet,
the nine of them
hanging in the barn for days,
halfway to growing wings.

When he couldn't stand it,
the sad, dumb look of them,
he led them to the coulee's edge
though they could barely walk
and shot them one by one.

His wife heard everything.
She met him halfway back,
took the rifle from his hands.

They still had the driving mare
and she'd hitched it up.
Without a word between them
they drove to town and sold the farm.
Just some packing up

and they'd be gone. Another house
with boarded windows.

Sometimes I feel we'll be
the last ones,
the preacher and his faithful
wife. Years later all these
stories no one wants to hear
pushing out of me
like big bleached bones
in silent meadows.
For the hay is withereth away,
the grass faileth,
there is no green thing.

COUNTING THE DAYS

Too many years of wanting
a child. Now I punch my belly
when the blood won't come.
Stupid, stupid woman!
Each day I pray for nothing.

This morning a faint
spot on my panties.
If I were sure
I'd hang them from the line,
this woman's sign of purity.

Paul won't drop by anymore
for fear of what Philip
may draw from his eyes. Yesterday
I saw him in Dawson's store.
You look weary, I said, and wanted
to smooth the worry lines away.
Weary, from the Anglo-Saxon,
meaning to walk across wet ground.
Stupid, stupid man. When will he shut up?

MRS. BENTLEY

I've walked through this story
in housedresses and splay-
footed rubbers. Mousy hair
without curls. Philip never drew
a convenient portrait
for me to comment on,
a hasty sketch. I could have said,
though his hand is flawless,
this does not resemble me.
That's my high forehead
and the way I purse my lips
but he's placed my eyes
far apart. I look in two directions.
The right one stares at you,
follows you as you move.
The left, my prairie eye,
gazes at what lies just over
where the lines converge.
No portraits exist, no photographs
and little self-description.
And nowhere in these pages

can you find my name.
Gladys, Louise, Madeline?
I fancy Margaret though in the country
everyone would call her Peg.
We're left with Mrs.
Bentley, dowdy, frumpy, plain.
Don't you wonder what Philip
called me as we lay together,
my flesh warmed by his hands,
the taste of me on his tongue,
as if there were no better sound
in all the world,
my name, my name!

STORM

Last night the wind blew
through town, an avenging angel
toppling cottonwoods and chicken coops,
levelling the stores' false fronts
with one sweep of its wings;
I cried above it, *I know the father*,
and Philip looked at me, my eyes
stripping everything away, the days
we hurt each other, my pettiness,
the terrible silences that clung to us
like dust. We held one another
and did not speak,
no need for words now, but a way to be
without dissembling, to move
into the fallen with the ease of light
claiming where a tree once stood,
a sudden opening in the heart
wind rushes through.

What if I had found another woman
said, *This is my life, these pieces,*
and she to me, like recipes exchanged
in some warm kitchen. Mrs. Bird perhaps
(is it Josephine?) washing a pail of saskatoons,
me rolling pastry for pie after pie,
how purple our speaking tongues.

What if I had held Judith
as a mother holds a child,
kisses her hair. I could have
said, *We have a little sister,*
and she hath no breasts:
what shall we do for our sister
on the day when she is spoken for?

What if I had found my own sound
on ivory skin, played the dark
notes too with the surest touch?

If I had found a friend,
if I had touched her –

behold thou art fair,
thou hast dove's eyes –
said this and this is my life,
not these scraps of gossip
we toss at one another
across a table set for tea,
nothing fit for anyone to eat.

O where are our fishes,
ye daughters of Jerusalem,
where are our pies, our mouths
plundered by berries,
where are our loaves of bread?

CALM

When the wind stops,
how strange it is –
everything as still
as the end of a concert
before applause
ripples the air.

The birds reel in
their singing.
The few dry leaves
settle into stillness.
Used to the keening of the wind
those of us on Main Street
pause, heads tilted,
as if trying to hear
someone softly speaking
in another room.

For one moment before
the dust grows wings,
I think of Paradise,

how this must feel
something like it.

Serene and at rest,
I seem to gleam
in my skin, waiting
on the other side of light
for the new
life to begin.

THE TRUTH

I would like to be innocent. I'm not,
though I'm not as bad as some
people make me. Consider the door,
the study, Philip's thin bitter mouth,
and what you would have done.
Think of our celebratory meal –
tinned salmon, the soft round
bones squished on the palate
with the tongue. I may have lied,
invented a future, a second story
with no stairs to take you there,
no landing.

Philip left the church,
we moved to the city.
But the bookstore I'd been dreaming of?
Can you imagine Philip among the shelves,
stocking the titles you have to sell
to survive? And what of the past, of Judith
and the baby, the convenient death?
Is any girl so dumb?

I love the detail of the oranges
I sent with Philip, pretending I didn't know.
It goes to show nothing can be innocent,
even an orange is pitted with meaning and intent.
So what's to be done with the larger things?

I could have lied –
I lied. There, I've said it,
but the most improbable is not
invention. The years and years of drought:
Joe Lawson's wife, the dead baby in the well,
the Chinaman who opened his door each night
to a woman's hunger. Everyone said
the grass would never grow again,
the sloughs never fill
and no one would come to love
this place. Even now as I write,
so long after, my pen makes
tracks across the dust.

If you'd like, I'll come clearer still.
Truth is, there never was a Judith.
Truth is, Philip is not the hero of

this story. Truth is, the only ending
is the one you make up, the one you can't
live without, the sweet, impossible birth.

Acknowledgements

I met Mrs. Bentley of Sinclair Ross's *As For Me and My House* when I was in my mid-twenties. She was the first literary character I'd encountered who inhabited the landscape where I was born. In some ways, I knew her instantly. Her ability to see the severe beauty of a countryside turned into desert was pure prairie; her sensibilities were shaped by wind, dust, and sky. One of the most enigmatic and controversial figures in Canadian literature, she has remained with me, particularly during the last ten years as I was writing these poems. The voice in her journals has been as hard to dispel from my imagination as a caragana rooted in soil.

Mrs. Bentley's journals, as well as numerous local histories, Barry Broadfoot's *Next-Year Country: Voices of Prairie People*, and Edward McCourt's *Saskatchewan* helped give me the flavour of the Depression era. As important were my mother's stories and the prodigious memory of my aunt, Gladys Hovde, who graciously tolerated my many questions. Jane Kerr's painting in AKA Gallery's

"The Farm Show" inspired the poem "Two Eternal Things," and the King James version of the Bible was a rich source of imagery. The last line of "A Man and a Woman" comes from the fifteenth-century anonymous poem "Western Wind."

I want to thank my companion, Patrick Lane, and my editor, Donna Bennett, who supported, encouraged, and challenged me in the writing of these poems. I also want to thank the University of Victoria as well as the B.C. Ministry of Small Business, Tourism and Culture for their financial support, and the Saskatchewan Writers'/Artists' Colony for providing me with a place on the prairies to write. Some of these poems appeared in *Geist* and *Prairie Fire*; the poem "Dust" was broadcast on CBC's "Morningside" as part of a Sinclair Ross memorial.

What Mrs. Bentley said of her husband, Philip, can be applied equally to the writer who brought her to life. Her words can be read as an acknowledgement of Ross's insurpassable genius: "I walked on, remembering how I used to think that only a great artist could ever paint the prairie, the vacancy and stillness of it, the bare essentials of a landscape, sky and earth, and how I used to look at Philip's work, and think to myself that the world would some day know of him."

It is my hope that Sinclair Ross, who died in Vancouver in early 1996, would have seen my interpretation of Mrs. Bentley as a tribute to the complexity and richness of his creation, and, finally, as a tribute to him.

A Man and a Woman / 1

In the Open / 2

Two Eternal Things / 4

Bumper Crop / 5

Cycles / 7

Country Dweller / 8

Names / 10

Dust / 13

Confession / 15

The Egg / 17

The Kind of Woman / 19

All the Room You Need / 22

Beauty / 23

Wind / 25

One Willow Grows / 27

The Painted Door / 28

Playing Liszt / 30

The Dance / 32

Burial, Partridge Hill / 34

Skinning Horses / 35

Not the Music / 37

Refrain / 39

Fox / 40

Garden / 41

Comfort Me / 43

Joe Lawson's Wife / 44

I Feed on Thistles / 48

State of Grace / 49

Sins of Omission / 51

Winter Horses / 52

Laughter Falls Like Rain / 53

What Words Are Left / 55

Judith / 57

Hawk and Rabbit / 61

Bag of Oranges / 62

This Is the Child / 65

Buffalo Stone / 67

Late Afternoon / 69

Paul / 71

How Beautiful Upon the Earth / 73

Isaiah 24:16 / 74

Mater Dolorosa / 75

Wilderness / 77

Leaving / 79

Counting the Days / 82

Mrs. Bentley / 83

Storm / 85

The First Supper / 86

Calm / 88

The Truth / 90